N. H. Claremont

Dedication of a Soldiers' Monument

N. H. Claremont

Dedication of a Soldiers' Monument

ISBN/EAN: 9783337134211

Printed in Europe, USA, Canada, Australia, Japan

Cover: Foto ©ninafisch / pixelio.de

More available books at **www.hansebooks.com**

DEDICATION

OF A

SOLDIERS' MONUMENT,

AT CLAREMONT, N. H.

OCTOBER 19, 1869.

PROCEEDINGS, SPEECHES, ETC.

CLAREMONT, N. H.:
PRINTED BY THE CLAREMONT MANUFACTURING CO.
1869.

DEDICATORY PROCEEDINGS.

In accordance with arrangements the ceremonies of dedicating a Soldiers'
Monument in Claremont, took place on the 19th of October A. D. 1869.
During the War of the Rebellion of 1861–65, when our Claremont Soldiers
were falling in the battles of Bull Run, Fair Oaks, Cold Harbor, Fredericksburg, the Wilderness and othe s, and dying in hospitals from disease induced
by hardships and exposure, it was determined that some suitable monument
should be erected in the town to commemorate the events of the war and perpetuate the memory and fame of those Claremont men who died while doing
battle for their country.

At the close of the war, in April, 1865, the Claremont Auxiliary Sanitary
Commission found in their treasury about one hundred and sixty dollars,
which by vote of the members was placed at interest as a Soldiers' Monument
fund, to be used when a sum should be obtained, which with this, would
pay for a suitable memorial to the fallen heroes of the town. About fifty
dollars were left after paying the expenses of a Fourth of July celebration,
in 1865, and this amount the committee of arrangements voted to appropriate
to the same object. At the annual town meeting, in March, 1867, it was
voted to appropriate one thousand dollars for a Soldiers' Monument, provided that five hundred dollars should be raised by contribution or otherwise.
Subscription papers, with a condition that no one should pay more than one
dollar, were circulated by ladies in each school district, and about six hundred
dollars were obtained. Heads of families generally paid one dollar, and children
of all ages twenty-five cents. Thus almost every individual at that time
in town contributed something towards this memorial, and there was not far
from eight hundred dollars obtained, besides the thousand dollars voted by the
town. At the annual town meeting, in March, 1868, it was voted to appropriate two thousand dollars to this object, provided that one thousand dollars
should be raised by contribution or otherwise. Samuel P. Fiske, Benjamin P.
Gilman, Edward L. Goddard, Charles H. Long and John L. Farwell were chosen

a committee to take charge of the whole matter and erect the monument. Subscription papers were circulated, without limiting the amount that each might pay, a dramatic exhibition given, and other means used to obtain the seven hundred dollars needed to make up the whole sum of fifteen hundred dollars to be contributed to make available the three thousand dollars voted by the town —making up the whole sum of forty-five hundred dollars. Many gentlemen subscribed very liberally, while others gave according to their means, and the required sum was assured.

The Committee made a contract, on very favorable terms, with the artist, Martin Milmore, of Boston, for the beautiful Monumental Statue, now standing upon the Park. When the monument and grounds were so nearly completed that a day could be fixed for the dedication, the Committee called a meeting of the citizens of the town, to be held at the Town Hall, on the evening of July 17, 1869, to take steps for the arranging and carrying out of proper exercises. At this meeting Edward L. Goddard was chosen chairman, and Hosea W. Parker, secretary. The following gentlemen were chosen a committee to take the whole subject of dedicating the monument in charge: Samuel P. Fiske, Benj. P. Gilman, Edward L. Goddard, Charles H. Long, John L. Farwell, Oscar J. Brown, John S. Walker, John F. Cossitt, Nathaniel Tolles, Hosea W. Parker, J. W. Peirce, Sherman Cooper, Henry Patten, Charles H. Eastman, William H. Nichols.

Subsequently, at a meeting of the Committee of Arrangements, it was voted to dedicate the Monument on the anniversary of the battle of Cedar Creek, October 19th, 1864, when Gen. Phil. H. Sheridan, by his timely arrival upon the field, changed a defeat of our arms into a glorious victory, taking fifty guns from the enemy. It was also voted to invite Dr. J. Baxter Upham, of Boston, a native of the town, to pronounce an oration. The Committee appointed the following officers for the day of dedication: President, John S. Walker; Vice Presidents, Edward L. Goddard, George N. Farwell, Samuel G. Jarvis, Albro Blodgett, Daniel W. Johnson, James P. Upham, Arnold Briggs, Daniel S. Bowker, Edward Ainsworth, Charles M. Bingham, William E. Tutherly, Sylvanus F. Redfield, William Ellis, Fred. P. Smith, Hiram Webb; Secretaries, Joseph Weber, Arthur Chase; Chaplain, Edward W. Clark; Marshal, Nathaniel Tolles,—who appointed for Assistants, Edwin W. Tolles, Edward J. Tenney, Sherman Cooper and George H. Stowell. He also appointed Otis F. R. Waite, Hosea W. Parker, William H. H. Allen and Francis F. Haskell, to receive and attend to the comfort of invited guests.

Invitations were extended by circulars to many prominent gentlemen, and by posters to the people generally, to be present and join in the ceremonies. The day arrived and was ushered in by a salute of thirty-seven guns and the ringing of bells at sunrise. It was one of those changeable days quite common in October—clouds, sunshine and squalls rapidly succeeding each other—yet a large concourse of people, variously estimated at from five to ten thousand, and among the number many distinguished ladies and gentlemen from the eastern and middle portions of the State, assembled to do honor to the occasion.

At half-past nine o'clock, A. M., the invited guests were met at the railroad station and conveyed in carriages to the village. At ten o'clock a procession, consisting of invited guests and officers of the day in carriages, fire companies, Posts of the Grand Army of the Republic, and citizens, was formed on the Common, under the direction of the Marshal, and, escorted by the Stearns Guards, of Claremont, headed by the Claremont Cornet Band, marched through Broad, North, Maple, Elm, Union, Sullivan, Pleasant, Summer and Broad streets, to the speaker's stand, at the east side of the Common, and facing the Monumental Statue to be dedicated. There was also a stand for the Band and Choir erected against the south wall of the Universalist church.

Arrived at the stand, the Band performed a national air. The Marshal, Nathaniel Tolles, called the assembly to order, and introduced Samuel P. Fiske, chairman of the Committee of Arrangements.

ADDRESS OF SAMUEL P. FISKE.

FELLOW CITIZENS: As chairman of a committee chosen by the town, in March, 1868, it devolves upon me to make a statement of the inception and progress of the work upon a Soldiers' Monument.

The idea of erecting, in some form, a lasting memorial to the brave men of Claremont who rushed to the rescue of the government when imperiled, and who laid down their lives in the cause of their country, originated—as good things often do—with the ladies.

When, in April, 1865, Gen. Grant brought the war of the rebellion to a sudden close, by the capture of Richmond and of Lee's army at Appomattox, the ladies of the "Auxiliary Sanitary Commission" had about one hundred and sixty dollars remaining in their treasury, which they voted should be placed at interest, to form a nucleus for a Soldiers' Monument fund. The amount was in various ways subsequently increased, though no decisive steps were taken until March, 1868, when the town, at its annual meeting, appropriated two thousand dollars, making with a former appropriation three thousand dollars, to be expended in the erection of a Soldiers' Monument, provided that one-half of that amount should be raised from other sources. At that meeting Samuel P. Fiske, Benj. P. Gilman, Edward L. Goddard, Charles H. Long and John L. Farwell, were chosen a committee to have charge of the matter, raise the money and erect the Monument.

The Committee, fellow-citizens, impressed with the belief that permanence and durability were indispensable, and that

"A thing of beauty is a joy forever,"

proceeded, with the limited funds at their disposal, to carry out what they believed to be the will of a large majority of the people interested.

After considering and rejecting many plans, they were fortunately placed in correspondence with Martin Milmore, of Boston, who, by reason of his devotion to art, conformed to their means, and they were enabled to contract for the beautiful, and, as they believe, most appropriate Memorial Statue, which we are assembled to-day to dedicate with fitting ceremonies.

Mr. Fiske announced the officers of the day, and introduced the President, John S. Walker, who said:

CITIZENS : Recognizing, as I trust we all do, the overruling hand of Providence in all our affairs, public and private, let us unite with the Chaplain, Rev. Mr. Clark, in the invocation of the divine blessing.

PRAYER BY REV. EDWARD W. CLARK.

Almighty God, our Heavenly Father, under this morning's light, we worship thee. In these beauties of nature around us we recognize the wonder-working hand of our Father. Thou art the inexhaustible source of all good, and we praise thee for thine excellent greatness. We call upon our souls, and all that is within us, to bless thy holy name. Command, we beseech thee, thy favor upon this day, this occasion, this assemblage of the people, and all the services of the hour. We own thee as ruler among the nations. Thou appointest the lot of all ; and we thank thee that the lines have fallen to us in such pleasant places, and that we have so goodly an heritage. We render thee thanks for our pleasant homes; our protection under just law, and for all our social and religious privileges. We praise thee for our happy form of government; for the ample domain of our country, affording refuge and homes to oppressed millions: for its plenteous products, crowning the year with goodness; for its works of invention and art; for its schools of instruction, scattering knowledge among all classes, and for the free possession and use of the holy scriptures. Father, we thank thee that when the arm of foes was raised in madness to strike down our beloved flag, and rend our Union of States, the loyal millions rose in defense, and thousands of patriotic hearts gave freely of wealth and life to save our land. Fathers and mothers gave sons, and wives husbands, and sisters brothers, to suffer and die for liberty. We praise thee for our regular army, and for our citizen-soldiery, who, led by noble and patriotic officers, went forth to conquer or to die. And we praise thee that, guided and protected by thy hand, they did conquer the foe, and now we have a country for the most part, united and at peace. We especially thank thee for those who went forth from this town, whose memory we cherish, and whose noble deeds and death in their country's service we this day celebrate, and erect a monument to their honor, and to perpetuate the remembrance of their toils, sacrifice and death for the land they loved. Bless the widows and orphans of our noble dead. Bless the soldiers of the Grand Army of the Republic, all over the land, and the Post established here, and those with us from abroad, who with equal love for country, toiled and sacrificed and exposed themselves to death, but who, protected by thy gracious hand, returned from the strife of battle to join with us in honoring their comrades. Guide these services. Let them kindle our hearts to a new flame of patriotic love and devotion. Aid thy servant who shall address us in memory of the dead, and may his words inspire us to all worthy thoughts and deeds. These things we do humbly ask through Jesus Christ, our Saviour. Amen!

ADDRESS OF THE PRESIDENT, JOHN S. WALKER.

Fellow Citizens: We have invited you to join with us in unveiling to-day a Statue in honor of the volunteer soldiers in the late war, living and dead, of and from Claremont.

We are happy to see that you have not delegated the acceptance of our invitation to a few representatives—but have come yourselves.

In the name of our people, whom the Committee represent, I bid you, each and all, a hearty, a cordial welcome. In considering how we could best give expression to our own feelings and our own sense of what would be suitable and appropriate in the way of ceremonies fitting to the occasion, we were unwilling to make our observance of them a merely local and town affair. Inasmuch as the Statue about to be unveiled is the embodiment of the form and spirit of patriotism familiar and common throughout the country, and wrought out by the artist, as we think, in a masterly, yet modest and beautiful fashion, we desired that our neighbors in other towns should look upon it as a memorial also of their heroic dead, and to appropriate it as fully as we do or can, as a sacred, enduring and hallowed memorial of the period to be forever pre-eminent in our national history, when they died that the Republic might live.

We desired that the honored Chief Magistrate of the Commonwealth, whose character and person are held in warmest respect, should lend dignity and grace to the occasion, by his presence. He scarcely needs to be assured how gladly we welcome him.

In the choice of a day for this inauguration, our minds could not but revert to that fearful, but most memorable, because grandly victorious day—of which this is the anniversary—the Battle of Cedar Creek. And, most naturally, we greatly desired the presence of him who turned that morning of disaster into an evening of joy and rejoicing —Gen. Phil. Sheridan. He accepted an invitation, and we had hoped and expected, until this morning, that he would have been with us. I am sure you will share the disappointment felt by the Committee at receiving a dispatch, saying it would be impossible for him to meet us to-day.

Chicago, Ill., Oct. 19, 1869.

J. S. Walker :—I telegraphed a few days ago to Gov. Stearns my inability to attend the dedication of the Soldiers' Monument at Claremont to-day, in consequence of the illness of Admiral Farragut in this city. Please say to my old comrades and the good people in attendance, how deeply I regret not being present with them to do honor to the memory of the gallant men from New Hampshire who fell in defense of the Union and their rights.

P. H. SHERIDAN,
Lieut. Gen.

To convince you, fellow citizens, how confidently we expected the presence of Gen. Sheridan, I will read to you his unqualified letter of acceptance:

Headquarters Military Division of the Missouri,)
Chicago, Sept. 22, 1869.)

Mr. J. S. Walker, Claremont, N. H.—My dear Sir :—Gen. Sheridan directs me to say that he accepts with pleasure the invitation of the citizens of Claremont to be present at the inauguration of a Soldiers' Monument, on the 19th of October next.

The delay in answering the invitation has been owing to the fact that the General did not know positively until to-day whether he could get away at that date.

He expects to accompany Gov. Stearns from Concord, as it is his intention to spend a day or two with him prior to the date named for the inauguration.

I am, sir, very respectfully, your ob't serv't,

GEO. A. FORSYTH,
Bvt. Brig. Gen. U. S. A., Mil. Sec.

It is, perhaps, enough for me to say that we did not entertain the shadow of a doubt that he would be present.

The reasons given in the dispatch I have read must be his excuse. But, gentlemen, the central figure of this occasion is yonder bronze, about to be unveiled, and we shall proceed with the ceremonies of the dedication, whether General Sheridan be here or elsewhere.

Fellow citizens, we have with us to-day some of our honored Senators and Representatives in Congress. We have many gentlemen eminent in military or civil life, or both, all of whom we cherish and welcome, and all of whom you shall have a chance to see and hear.

I am detaining you too long from the rarer dishes of the feast. It only remains for me to say,—let the statue which we have erected, to stand in sunshine and in storm, from generation to generation, the instruction, the admonition, the admiration of our children and our children's children, the testimony and memorial of the patriotism and the sacrifices of the Volunteer Soldiers in the late war, be now unveiled.

The signal being given, the American flag, which had enveloped the bronze Statue, was skillfully lifted therefrom by Samuel P. Fiske, chairman of the Monument Committee, assisted by Benj. P. Gilman, raised to the top of the pole, and floated in the breeze over the Monument. The roaring of cannon, rolling of drums, cheers of the crowd, and the "Star Spangled Banner," sung by the Choir, accompanied by the Band, greeted the splendid effigy of that noblest of characters, the Citizen Soldier.

The President introduced the Orator, Dr. J. Baxter Upham, of Boston, a native of Claremont.

DR. UPHAM'S ORATION.

"The whole land," said Pericles, the matchless Grecian orator, speaking in commemoration of the Athenian dead, "the whole land is the sepulchre of illustrious men."

This was spoken, more than two thousand years ago, of that staunch and loyal little Republic,—"the land of popular liberty,—the home of letters and of arts," strong in its love of the right, brave of heart, invincible in spirit, but whose geographical area, in comparison with our own vast domain, is as that of an acre to the largest limits of a State. And now, after so long a lapse of ages, can it not, with equal significance, be said of this fair Republic? Founded in a brave resistance to foreign usurpation and aggression, maintained under the jealousy and covert antagonism of the kingly powers of Europe, passing unharmed through minor wars and disturbances, it has, in these latter days of its comparatively brief existence, been called upon to suffer and to put down the most wicked, as it was the most determined and obstinate, and, may I not add, the mightiest and most stupendous rebellion the world has yet seen. Yes,—the whole land may now be called a sepulchre of the illustrious dead. They lie in every field and forest, on the banks of rivers, under the shadows of the solemn hills, by the shores of the sea and in its unsounded depths, in the quiet graveyards of every town and village and hamlet,—and their presence pervades and sanctifies the earth, the air, and the sea.

Standing here, under this gray October sky, near the spot where I was born, on an occasion at once so novel and so impressive, before these high dignitaries of the State, these hero-representatives of our armies, in the presence of this vast multitude who have come up hither from all parts of the old county of Cheshire, and from more distant towns,—many of whom are known to me from my childhood,—a crowd of tender recollections comes rushing back upon my brain.

"The outward world around us remains indeed the same. The same nature—undying, undecayed"—is here. But all else, how changed! As I look out upon these scenes, so familiar and dear to me,—this amphitheatre among the hills, the solemn Ascutney, the meadow and its winding river, to swim in whose waters and skate upon whose glassy surface was a part of my early education, the

site of the old school-house and the church, these plains
and valleys, and fertile fields, calm and peaceful as of old,
I can with difficulty bring to myself the reality that some
of those who joined with me here in the sports of boyhood
have passed through the maddening carnage of civil
war, and I now read their names on yonder tablets—that
martyr list of heroes.

But if, amid all the changes, political and social, which
must needs happen in a quarter of a century and more of
one's life, it had been possible to foresee that "great trial
and great task of our liberty" through which we have just
gone, I could have also foreseen, to a certainty, that the
part my native town should bear in it would be just the
honorable record it has shown. The military history of
the State justifies this. The chronicles of the town, from
its first settlement in 1762, have given a warrant and a
pledge of it. For among the earliest settlers I find the
names of Joseph Waite—(whether or not an ancestor of
our respected fellow-citizen of that name, to whom we are
all so much indebted for his valuable and painstaking history of our Claremont soldiers in the recent struggle, I
cannot say)—Col. Joseph Waite, who, on the authority of
Mansfield, the annalist, had already won distinction in the
French and Indian war, was a captain in Rogers' famous
corps of Rangers in 1759, and commanded a regiment in
the war of the Revolution.—Capt. Joseph Taylor, who, in
1755, was taken by the Indians and sold to the French,
but escaped and took part in the siege of Louisburg, and
afterward in the Revolutionary struggle, and died at the
good old age of 84, in 1813.—Hon. Samuel Ashley, a man
of note in our annals, who had served with credit in the
old French war, and filled many offices of civil trust in the
town, and others of like distinction, who might be named
if the time would permit. And immediately upon the
outbreak of hostilities in 1775, I find the names of several
of our citizens upon the muster rolls of the First New

Hampshire Regiment,—that honored Regiment which, under the gallant Stark, was conspicuous at Bunker Hill, and which followed the varying fortunes of the patriot army till the final capitulation at Yorktown. The men of Claremont bore their part also in the second war with England, on the fields where Miller and McNeil so nobly upheld the honor of the State. In later struggles,—in Texas, under Houston, one life from here, at least, went down to its unknown grave. Nor were the Florida and Mexican wars without their representatives from this devoted town.

So, when the news came that treason and rebellion had burst forth into actual hostilities on that memorable 12th day of April, 1861, true to the old honor and name, the citizens of Claremont, with one accord, sprang to meet the issue. I need not recall to your minds with what alacrity the whole community came together, each vieing with the other in encouraging enlistments and furnishing that material aid which has well been called " the sinews of war "—pledging, if need be, in the spirit and language of the Revolutionary fathers, " their lives, their fortunes, and their sacred honor,"—womanly hands, too, taking up the good work and laboring earnestly and unceasingly for the same noble end—all this is still fresh in your memories.

Within three days from the President's proclamation and call for seventy-five thousand men to suppress a rebellion against the government of the United States, and immediately upon the order issued by the Governor for a regiment to be raised in this State to serve for three months, an office was opened here for enlistments; " the young men," says your historian, " flocked in faster than they could be examined and sworn." On the 30th of the same month, Major Waite set forth, with the eighty-five patriot soldiers recruited by Capt. Austin, for the rendez- vous of the regiment at Concord,—a full company nearly,

from this town of about four thousand inhabitants,—
and, if the whole population of the State had been repre-
sented in the same ratio, instead of a single regiment of
seven hundred and eighty rank and file, enough for more
than ten regiments could have been had on this first
call to arms. As it was, more than enough for two regiments volunteering, the Claremont men were sent to Ports-
mouth, where, at the second call of the President, on the
3d of May, for three hundred thousand men for three
years, one-half of this company at once re-enlisted, the
remainder being discharged for disability or sent to the
defense of the sea-coast at Fort Constitution. This was
the first offering of some of its noblest representatives sent
forth by this town to battle with the Rebellion. They
could have been urged by no other than the purest motives of patriotism—with no prospect of reward save the
proud consciousness of doing their duty.

This regiment, in which they finally enlisted, was vir-
tually the First of the New Hampshire regiments in the
war of the Rebellion, though still retained as the Second
in the nomenclature of the New Hampshire line—first,
as it was, at least, coeval in its organization with the
three months' regiment which preceded it, by a little, to
the field of strife,—first, as it had the priority in its actual
baptism of fire and of blood. Not to lay undue stress
upon this point, I may be pardoned for dwelling somewhat on the exploits of this gallant regiment, from the
circumstances I have already named, and from the fact
that it was my proud good fortune, at the head of a
thousand Sons of New Hampshire, to welcome its full
ranks as it passed through Boston, on its way to Washington, on the 20th of June, 1861; and therefore I have
followed its onward career with a more than ordinary
interest. It alone, among the regiments of our State,
participated in the first great battle of Bull Run, doing all,
under its brave leaders, that valor and determination could

do to breast the woful disasters of that day—giving,
in the death of Andrew J. Straw, of this town, the first
New Hampshire martyr to freedom, slain in battle, in this
war. The loss of the regiment in killed and wounded
was severe. Its gallant Colonel was stricken down at the
head of his command, early in the action, but returned
and continued in the fight. It went into the fray with
full ranks and buoyant spirits. It came out of it with at
least equal honor with any other of that patriot army,
which then and there learned the stern but salutary lesson of a first defeat. Its next experience was at the siege
of Yorktown, and, immediately afterwards, at the san-
guinary battle of Williamsburg, where it fought with
honor and with varying success, with the loss of about
one hundred men. We hear of it next at Fair Oaks and
Malvern Hill, and in most of the bloody battles of the
memorable seven days' fight and retreat to the James
River. The following year, after consecrating itself anew
to the cause at the second Bull Run, where it behaved
with distinguished gallantry, losing ten of its twenty-one
commissioned officers, and one hundred and thirty-two
of the little more than three hundred rank and file with
which it entered the fight, it encamped at night on the
identical spot where it formed its first line of battle in
1861. Thence its route was direct to Chantilly and Fredericksburg, in which last it found in the General-in-chief
of the Army, its tried and faithful leader under whom,
as Colonel commanding a brigade, it had fought at the
first Bull Run. In the memorable battle of Gettysburg
its gallantry was conspicuous, suffering a loss, in killed
and wounded, of a majority of its field and line officers
and more than one-half of its rank and file. The next year
finds the regiment engaged in the action at Drury's Bluff—
the battles of Cold Harbor and second Fair Oaks, and the
siege of Petersburg. This was after it had returned to
New Hampshire, been reorganized, had incorporated into

its ranks the residue of the 17th, a nine months' regiment, and otherwise recruited its shattered forces and come back with a renewed vigor to the scene of conflict. The regiment was subsequently in several skirmishes, and minor engagements, losing heavily in the aggregate—took part, under Butler, in the defense of Bermuda Hundred—and, on the 3d of April, 1865, entered the city of Richmond and encamped on its outskirts, amid the smoke and cinders of the burning capital. Here it remained till after the surrender at Appomattox. It was not till the 26th of December following that the corps was finally paid off and disbanded, having enlisted earlier and remained later in the field than any other permanent organization from the State.

"The Roll of this regiment," writes one of its field officers, "presents, since its organization, a list of more than three thousand names. Every regiment from New Hampshire, with two exceptions, has been supplied, in part, with officers from its ranks. The rosters in more than thirty regiments in the field contain the names of those who were once identified with it. It has marched six thousand miles, participated in more than twenty pitched battles, and lost in action upwards of one thousand men."

I have already alluded to the First New Hampshire regiment in the war of the Revolution. On looking carefully into its history, I am struck with the remarkable parallel between that and the regiment we have just been considering. Go back with me over the intervening period of nearly a hundred years and attest to the truth of this. In that war New Hampshire maintained three full regiments in the field, called the 1st, 2d and 3d of the New Hampshire Line. Besides these, there were others which served under a militia organization, for brief periods and at various

times, as emergencies required. Two days after the attack
of the British forces upon our troops at Lexington, a con-
vention of delegates assembled at Exeter to take meas-
ures " to assist our suffering brethren in the Province of
Massachusetts Bay and to order the necessary supplies
for the troops." Immediately the men of New Hampshire were on their way to Cambridge, where they were
organized in two regiments under the already famous
John Stark of Londonderry, and James Reed of the
county of Cheshire. They went into camp at Medford,
the former with twelve, the latter with ten full companies. " On the day of the battle of Bunker Hill," says
Frothingham, " about the time when the British army
had landed, the New Hampshire regiments under Stark
and Reed arrived from Medford. Stark had marched at
a leisurely pace over the Neck, which was swept by the
fire of the floating batteries of the enemy, ' because,' as
he said to his commanding General, ' one fresh man in
action is better than ten who are exhausted.'" I need
not recount the deeds of these men of New Hampshire
on that eventful day. They were posted, as you know,
at the historical *rail-fence*, where the battle raged the
fiercest and the British dead were strown the thickest—
and, as they were among the first of the re-enforcements
to arrive, so, with ammunition spent, outnumbered by
more than ten to one of the hostile forces, they were the
last to take up the reluctant retreat. In 1776, Stark was
ordered on the expedition to Canada, and, on his return,
formed, with his regiment, a part of Gen. Sullivan's Brigade, under the command of Washington, at Philadelphia.
Remaining, at the special entreaty of Washington, after
the term of their enlistment had expired, the regiment
shortly afterward took a brilliant and glorious part in the
battles of Trenton and of Princeton—how important will
appear when we remember that, of the three divisions of
the army, directed to cross the river and attack the ene-

my at Trenton, that containing the New England troops
alone succeeded in effecting a passage. Gen. Sullivan,
with the brigade of New Hampshire soldiers, was the first
to commence the attack. Col. Stark, with his regiment,
led the right wing and, as Wilkinson writes, "dealt death
wherever he found resistance, and bore down all opposi-
tion before him." At Princeton, too, "no regiment," we
are told, "was more conspicuous than that commanded
by Col. Stark." We find it next at Saratoga, where, on
the 7th of October, 1777, under Col. Cilley, the successor
of Stark, it did much in aid of that signal success of our
arms which led, on the 17th of the same month, to the
surrender of Burgoyne with his army. It was here the
New Hampshire troops several times took and retook the
cannon of the enemy, driving all before them. We can
not stop to follow minutely the brilliant career of the regiment from this time onward; it appears again with its
victorious banner at Bennington and at Bemis' Heights—
we find it foremost in the pursuit of the enemy's retreat-
ing columns at Monmouth Court House—we see it
throwing up intrenchments on the rugged heights at Still-
water—we trace its bloody footsteps on the snows of that
terrible winter at Valley Forge—we hail it exultingly,
under Scammel and Dearborn, in the siege and surrender
at Yorktown—and we bid it a tender and affectionate
farewell when, on that 1st of January, 1784, the war long
since over, after eight years and eight months of continu-
ous and most arduous service, its scarred veterans rest
finally from the labor of arms and return to their peaceful
homes.

It is interesting to note the similarity in the fortunes of
these two regiments separated by an interval of almost a
hundred years. Both were coeval in their organization
with the commencement of the war—both were engaged
with honor in the first great struggle of their respective
campaigns—both were prominent in most of the decisive

battles—both conspicuous for bravery of commanders and
men—both present, or at least within sound of the guns,
at the final surrender; both also prolonged their term of
service beyond the usual period—both were the last, or
among the very last, to lay down their arms and return
to their homes. Are not these significant facts? Do
they not teach us that history has not gone backward—
the heroic age has not passed away—the sons of New
Hampshire are not degenerate—the children of to-day are
able and willing and worthy to accept and maintain the
glorious legacy of their sires?

New Hampshire gave to the country, in this last trial
of her faith, the services of eighteen regiments of infantry—fourteen for three years or the war, one for three
months, three for nine months, of which one was subsequently merged in a former and more enduring organization—a full regiment of cavalry—a regiment of heavy,
and a battery of light artillery—and three companies of
sharp-shooters, beside its representatives in several of
the regiments from other States, and its full quota for
the Navy.

The regiment I have designated, and whose record I
have dwelt upon somewhat, is but the type of all the rest.
By several indeed it has been surpassed in the severity of
hardships endured, and the fearful sacrifices made in
hospitals and in the field; the Third, the Fifth, the Sixth,
the Seventh, the Ninth and the Fourteenth Infantry, the
regiment of Cavalry, the Artillery and the several companies of Sharp-shooters, contained each their full quota
of Claremont men, and, as their brave officers here can
attest, were mostly in the hardest and thickest of the fight.
The mere mention of their battles would form a catalogue
too long for enumeration. Their field of operations cov-
ered almost the whole battle-ground of the Rebellion;
they fought with McDowell, with McClellan, with Burn-
side, with Hooker, with Meade, with Banks, with Foster,

with Sherman, with Sheridan, with Grant; in the East,
in the West, in the South; in the Carolinas, in Florida,
in Louisiana, in Arkansas, in Kentucky, in Tennessee—
in the Army of the Potomac, of the James, of the Cum-
berland, of the Mississippi, of the Gulf—but chiefly, to
their good fortune be it known, and first and last, in that
glorious though much abused old *Army of the Potomac*—
of which so much has been said, and justly said, in
praise, of which much also, in the dark days of our country's bitterest trial and almost desperation, too much,
alas! has been said in disparagement and derision—"that
much suffering old army," as the gallant and eloquent
General Chamberlain has said of it, "scoffed at for not
moving, but never, that he had heard of, for not dying
enough—*wonderful old army* whose casualties were such
that decimation were five times too tame a word to tell
its losses; an army sometimes changing its base, and often
its commanders, but never its loyalty and its steadfast
devotion—*self-denying old army*, so often held back from
following up the victory, because it *was* the Army of the
Potomac and must not uncover Washington—schooled
in the passive no less than in the active virtues, disciplined
in patience, in fortitude, in self-control; ready to lay
down their arms at the feet of the constitutional authority
with as much sincerity, as much humility, as they had
seen in the hostile host that had laid down at their feet
the arms and colors of its lost cause."

On the marble tablets in yonder Town Hall—which
from henceforth shall be a memorial hall as well—we
may trace the names of SEVENTY-THREE young men who
fought in these armies and voluntarily laid down their
lives upon the altar of their country—more than a seventh part of the four hundred and forty-nine who from
first to last enlisted here—so many, alas! in number, that
there is not room for them upon the entablature of this or

any common monument. I could wish it were possible to write them, one and all, in letters of living light, on the sides of these everlasting hills, that they might be known and read of all men. Suffer me reverently to speak to you some of these familiar names.

Col. ALEXANDER GARDINER, commanding the Fourteenth Regiment—the model of a faithful, efficient officer, the scholarly and accomplished gentleman. Capt. Wm. Henry Chaffin, acting Lieut. Col. of his Regiment, and Lieut. Henry S. Paull—both brave and true men, killed at the same time that their beloved commander was mortally wounded, at the battle of Opequan Creek, near Winchester, on the 19th day of September, 1864— over whose remains, with others slain in that memorable engagement, a grateful State has placed a monument on the field.

Lieut. Ruel G. Austin, mortally wounded at the battle of Gettysburg.

Lieut. Charles O. Ballou, "whose memory shall be kept," wrote the Captain of his Company, "so long as the banner of the glorious Fifth continues to wave."

Lieut. Robert Henry Chase, "than whom New Hampshire has sent no braver man to the field," said the commanding officer of his Regiment.

Lieut. Samuel Brown Little, stricken down in the thickest of the fight at Antietam, and, though still disabled, hastening to Fredericksburg, to receive there his mortal wound.

Lieut. George Nettleton, whose last words to his wife were—"If I fall, remember it was at the post of duty and in a noble cause."

Lieut. Wm. Danford Rice—"too well known and loved for any words of mine to add to or detract," wrote Lieut. Col. Whitfield of him.

Serg't Luther A. Chase, Serg't Horatio C. Moore, Serg't Edward F. Moore, Serg't Ard Scott, Serg't George

E. Rowell, Serg't Charles W. Wetherbee,—"DEAD ON
THE FIELD OF HONOR."

I have thus read, in your hearing, in the order of their
military rank, a few of the well known names that form
that Roll of Immortality—dear and cherished amongst
you every one. I wish it were permitted me to add to
this shining list the honored name of Major Charles
Jarvis, who, though not of us, is endeared to us by so
many familiar associations—endeared especially to some
now present who served under him during his brief, yet
glorious career;—but our sister town, just over the river,
claims his precious dust.

> "Green be the turf above thee,
>   Friend of my better days ;
> None knew thee but to love thee,
>   Nor named thee but to praise."

There remains unread a still larger list of the honored
dead—equally high on the martyr roll of fame; indeed it
is the peculiar feature of this war that in the rank and
file of the patriot army are to be found instances innu-
merable of heroic daring—of devotion, of self-sacrifice
and christian patriotism—that can hardly be paralleled
in the annals of war in all the world. To name two or
three only of such instances : Take young Putnam of
the Second, who in the hurried and disastrous retreat
of the first Bull Run, found time to go out of his way to
visit his wounded associates in the hospital, and to get
water for his dying comrades, under the storm of the
enemy's shot and shell—of whom his commanding officer wrote, "his kindness and manly bearing had taught
me to love him like a brother;" and Neal of the Third,
whose last regret was that "he had but one life to give
to his country;" and Hart of the Fifth, Charles A. Hart,
who, when mortally wounded and left upon the field, did
just what immortalized the name of Sir Phillip Sidney at

the battle of Zutphen—declined the proffered aid to himself in favor of another at his side who seemed to him to need it more. But I forbear. My excellent friend, the Chaplain here, could tell you, I doubt not, of a hundred like instances of noble and manly devotion to duty and to humanity, which the exercise of his sacred functions in hospital and on the field has privileged him to know. He could tell you of such tender and touching words committed by dying lips to his keeping—such instances of exalted patriotism—such love of kindred and of friends—such high and holy faith—such yearnings after the higher good—such aspirations for heaven breathed out by these young lives in death as, clothed in the garb of poesy and song, would stir our souls as with the music of a mighty symphony.

The question very naturally arises just here—as it has arisen and been answered a hundred times already on occasions like this — Why all this outpouring of precious blood? Was the end gained worth the untold sacrifice it cost? Are the objects secured worthy of these hecatombs of human lives which have been offered up so freely in every city and village and hamlet throughout the land? We cannot stop now to discuss the origin and causes of this gigantic rebellion; nor is there need of it: they are well known to the oldest and the youngest before me. I will only recall to you the words of the archleaders themselves of the great conspiracy, to show that they well knew they were plotting treason against the fairest and best government on the face of the earth, and that, in spite of all their assertions to the contrary, they stand convicted, from out of their own mouths, of a parricidal determination to subvert that government, in order to serve their own selfish ends. As late as November, 1860, Alexander H. Stephens, afterward Vice-President of the so-called Confederacy, speaking of the heritage handed down to us by our

fathers, called it "the most beneficent government of
which history gives us any account." Jefferson Davis,
from his seat in the U. S. Senate, during that very winter when secession was brewing in the South, declared
it to be "the best government ever instituted by man,
unexceptionably administered, and under which the
people have been prosperous beyond comparison with
any other people whose career has been recorded in history." Yet Mr. Everett tells us that, in that winter of
1860–61, within his own personal knowledge, it was
admitted in substance, by one of the most influential
leaders of secession, that, because, for the first time
since the adoption of the constitution, an election of
President had been effected without the votes of the
South, the rebellion was to be commenced by the occu-
pation of the national capital, with the seizure of the
public archives and of the treaties with foreign powers;
and it was fondly thought that this object could be
effected by a bold and sudden movement, on the 4th of
March, 1861. God be praised that by the prudent fore-
thought and preparation of the veteran chief then in
command of our slender military force, this foul conspiracy was for the moment frustrated and so dire a national
disgrace and calamity averted! It was therefore in the
spirit of hatred and revenge—for the wicked and unlaw-
ful assumption of the power into their own hands—that
these leaders of the rebellion were willing to destroy
that "beneficent government," and drench their fair
land, if need be, with the blood of half a million of its
sons. For this they fired upon their country's flag when
the "Star of the West" attempted to relieve the fam-
ishing garrison in Charleston harbor. For this they
declared in their so-called confederate congress, at Mont-
gomery, that, before the end of May, their secession
banner should be planted on the dome of the Capitol at
Washington. For this they precipitated the savage

attack upon Sumter and its devoted band, and forced
upon the reluctant North a war which, for the magni-
tude of its proportions and the extent of its field of
operations, has no parallel in history.

But *the results*—THE RESULTS: are they commensurate
with such fearful sacrifices? This is the question
which continually recurs to us, and which these silent
memorials, springing up all over the land, will be ever
reminding us of. What then are some of the results
obtained? Imagine for a moment what would have been
our condition to-day if we had failed of success; if we
had not, by the continued recruiting of our armies, "op-
posed force to force so long as a vestige of hostile force
remained;" if we had not urged the chalice of direful
war prepared by our misguided brethren of the South
to their own lips and made them drink it to the bitter
dregs. No words of mine can paint the picture with
anything like an adequate coloring. I borrow the words
of Mr. Everett, in his masterly oration at the consecration
of the National Cemetery at Gettysburg, in November,
1863 (this before the war was decided, remember), when
I say that "on the issue depends whether or not this
august republican Union, founded by some of the wisest
statesmen that ever lived, cemented with the blood of
some of the purest patriots that ever died, should perish
or endure. * * * * To yield to the demands of the
South and acknowledge its independence, thus resolving
the Union at once into two hostile governments, with a
certainty of further disintegration, would annihilate the
strength and influence of the country as a member of
the family of nations; afford to foreign powers the opportunity and the temptation for humiliating and disastrous influence in our affairs; wrest from the Middle
and Western States some of their great natural outlets
to the sea, and of their most important lines of internal
communication; deprive the commerce and navigation

of the country of two-thirds of our sea coast and of the
fortresses which protect it; not only so, but would en-
able each individual state to cede its territory, its harbors,
its fortresses, the mouths of its rivers to any foreign
powers. It cannot be," he concludes, "that the people
of the loyal states will, for the temptation of a brief
truce in an eternal border-war, consent to this hideous
national suicide."

As to the positive benefits that have accrued—they
are more and greater than can be told in the brief time
at my command. "That these young men threw themselves promptly and heartily into the war," says Higgin-
son, "and that not in recklessness and bravado, not
merely won by the dazzle of a uniform, or allured by
the charm of personal power, or controlled by 'that last
infirmity,' ambition—but evidently governed, above all
things else, by a solid conviction of duty and of right
—to have established incontestably this one point, is
worth the costly sacrifice which completed the demon-
stration." But more than this,—we have earned a
name and a fame in history such as no other nation on
the earth can surpass. Not republican Greece or Rome
in their palmiest days, can furnish a brighter record of
patriotism. Not Marathon or Thermopylæ, or Pharsa-
lia, or Marengo, or Waterloo can bring witness of
bloodier or more sternly contested battles. Against
Miltiades, against Cæsar, against Wellington, against
Ney, against Nelson, we presume to place our Grant,
our Sherman, our Meade, our Sheridan, our Farragut.
Think you if that illustrious charge had been made by
Americans instead of by Frenchmen, under the leadership of our *Marshal Ney*, the triple wall of English bayonets even, could have long withstood the impetuous
onset?

This war has taught us to trust in our own resources,
and not lean too confidingly on the faith and friend-

ship of any foreign nation, even if it be our own kindred and blood. It has taught us to rely, under God, on the strong right arm of the people—on that intelligence and sense of honor and of justice and right which pervades the great mass of our citizens, whether native born or adopted; that, however much smaller issues may at times divide and distract us, there exists deeper down a great undertow of loyalty and of patriotism that will always and surely bring us out right in the end. It has shown to us the real meaning and significance of independence in its fullest and largest sense. It has given to us, at last, a liberty which is the substance and synonym of *freedom*. And it has given back to us, in its entirety and its integrity, in all its comeliness and goodly proportions and vast extent, without compromise or reserve, beyond all question and controversy in the future, OUR COUNTRY! Is not this worth the cost, my friends—yes! even the cost of all these dear and precious ones you have been called to offer up in death?

> " O, Beautiful ! MY COUNTRY ! ours once more !
> Smoothing thy gold of war-dishevelled hair
> O'er such sweet brows as never other wore,
> What were our lives without thee?
> What *all* our lives to save thee?
> We reck not what we gave thee ;
> We will not dare to doubt thee ;
> Bow down, dear Land, for thou hast found release !
> Bow down in Prayer and Praise ;
> Thy God, in these distempered days,
> Hath taught thee the sure wisdom of His ways,
> And THROUGH THINE ENEMIES *hath wrought thy peace.*"

Let us turn, for a moment, to the contemplation of this memorial structure which you have reared in grateful acknowledgment of the deeds of the patriotic dead. As it emerged just now from its drapery of flags, amid the salutation of cannon and martial music and the plaudits of this vast multitude, I hailed it as the fittest

and purest symbol of all this endurance and suffering
and sacrifice. I see in its manly form and calm and
restful *pose*, the trusting, thoughtful, brave, intelligent
citizen soldier of the Republic. I congratulate the
youthful artist here upon his happily conceived design—
so nobly planned, so successfully accomplished. I congratulate the committee of my fellow citizens upon the
consideration and good taste they have shown in the
execution of their delicate trust. I congratulate the
town of my nativity on the possession of so noble and
beautiful a work of art. More than all I rejoice with
the bereaved ones before me that, in this almost living,
breathing bronze, they may, each for themselves, behold
again the image of their martyred dead.

There stands in the middle of Place Vendome, in
Paris, a column of grand and lofty proportions, made
from the iron and bronze of captured cannons, and surmounted by the statue of the first Napoleon. At night-
fall the veteran survivors of those memorable campaigns
come and sit down and weep around this statue—it may
be with thoughts of the departed glory of their great
hero, it may be with recollections of his fruitless victories. Not so with this emblem of your departed braves.
Yours is cause for joy and exultation rather than grief;
yours the saying of that Spartan mother who through
her tears could yet exclaim—"I would not exchange
my dead son for any living one upon the earth:" yours
a heritage better than wealth, better than titled honors,
better than coronets bestowed by kings and emblazoned
on books of heraldry.

The pyramids cover the dust of once mighty po-
tentates, whose very names are forgotten. The solemn Sphynx still looks out over the vast plains of
Egypt, but why it was reared or what it commemorates
none can tell. Memnon lies shattered and half buried
in the sand, and its music has no voice for us. But the

name and significance of this memorial shaft shall never
be forgotten; the comparatively fragile structure may
indeed disappear,—its bronze corrode and the granite
crumble away, but when those mute lips shall have
ceased to utter their eloquent lesson to generations yet
unborn, the memory of this hour shall be still green—
the light of this hour shall shine along the pathway of
the ages so long as time endures.

My friends and fellow citizens—my part of the sad
yet grateful duty of this day—oh! how inadequately
indeed!—is accomplished.

Surviving heroes!—who so freely offered yourselves
to death and yet live—to you and your children and
your children's children, belongs the legacy of this
goodly day.

Spirits of the heroic dead!—slain in battle, or dead
of wounds or disease, of exposure or starvation—martyrs
to your country and to liberty,—if from your serene
abode it be permitted you to take cognizance of things
here,—to you and to your beloved memory we dedicate this offering of our admiration and our love. Nay,
rather, in the undying words of our martyr President,
"it is altogether fitting and proper that we should do
this thing. But, in a larger sense, we cannot dedicate
—we cannot consecrate—we cannot hallow the ground
where rests our heroic dead. It is for us, the living,
rather to be dedicated to the work they have so nobly
achieved. It is rather for us to take from these honored
dead, increased devotion to the cause for which they
gave the last full measure of devotion; to highly resolve
that the dead shall not have died in vain—that this great
nation shall, under God, have a new birth of freedom,
and that the government of the people, by the people
and for the people, shall not perish from the earth."

After the oration, "America" was sung by the Choir, under the leadership of Moses R. Emerson.

THE PRESIDENT.—I am happy to say to you fellow citizens, that Governor Stearns, who has honored our dedication with his presence, can make as good a speech as the President of the United States, Gen. Grant, could, if he were here himself. (Great laughter and cheers as the Governor came forward.)

REMARKS OF GOVERNOR ONSLOW STEARNS.

MR. PRESIDENT, LADIES AND GENTLEMEN: I thank you for your kind and cordial greeting. It affords me great pleasure to express my sympathy with the effort by which this monument, so appropriate in its design and so excellent in its execution, has been completed; and with every effort by which it is sought to express in enduring form the gratitude we owe to those who sacrificed their lives in the defense and for the preservation of our country.

While we honor the memory of the dead by monuments and memorials, we should also remember our duty to the survivors whom the fortunes of war have rendered deserving objects of our sympathy and aid.

We have especial cause to be proud of the part which New Hampshire soldiers sustained in the late war. They bore our colors with firmness and courage in whatever positions they were placed, and their history is a bright record of honorable deeds. Among them all none were more worthy than those whose memory we now seek to honor.

But after the appropriate words of eulogy that have been uttered in your hearing, it is not needful that I should speak at length. The occasion itself is eloquent, and the beautiful statue before you has a voice above all human speech. I regret that the honored chief under whose leadership so many of New Hampshire citizen-soldiers were proud to serve, is absent from this commemorative service. General Sheridan is detained by the illness of the gallant Farragut, whose imperishable fame is the common glory of his country.

With renewed assurances of my gratification and sympathy, I thank you for your attention and kindness.

THE PRESIDENT.—We have with us to-day a gentleman whom you have often heard before, and to whom you always listen with pleasure—Ex-Gov. Harriman (Cheers.)

SPEECH OF EX-GOV. WALTER HARRIMAN.

MR. PRESIDENT AND FELLOW CITIZENS: I am not the orator of the occasion and I shall therefore say but little. The oration—and an admirable one it was—has been pronounced. You have also listened to the appropriate words of His Excellency, and I need say but little.

You dedicate, to-day, by these imposing ceremonies, yonder splendid monument. There it stands, and there for ages it will remain, sacred to the memory of your dead—attesting your munificence and your patriotism.

Braver men never faced danger than those whose deeds are commemorated by that noble statue. Our citizen-soldiery took high rank on the roster of heroes, and wherever death spread his banquet, New Hampshire furnished many guests. I see before me not a few of the war-worn veterans who endured the hardships and braved the dangers of the great conflict, but alas! many of their comrades are not here. Their marches, their sieges and their conflicts have passed into history; and while we mourn their departure we would gratefully welcome to our hearts the cheering consolations of the Christian faith,—

> "There is no death! what seems so is transition;
>   This life of mortal breath
> Is but the suburb of the life elysian,
>   Whose portal we call death.
>
> In that great cloister's stillness and seclusion,
>   By guardian angels led;
> Safe from temptation, safe from sin's pollution,
>   They live whom we call dead."

In the presence of their speechless but eloquent dust; in the presence of the doubting and sneering foreign enemies of free government; in the presence of oppressed millions of other lands, who, when the sable curtains of night seemed to hang over a doomed nation, watched our flag with tears: in the presence of a God of justice, we stand pledged to maintain and perpetuate the beneficent government which they died to save!

God was with our soldiers, for they were striking chains from His children. The blood they shed was sacred, for they died that the Union might survive: that manhood might be disinthralled; that groping, downtrodden humanity might have a glorious resurrection; that this nation, the favorite child of Divine Providence, clothed with new vigor and beauty, might be raised to a purer and higher civilization than it had known before.

In the grand future that lies before us, when this nation shall count upon its census roll three hundred millions of intelligent and liberty-loving people,—when it shall become the evangelizer of the world, the disenthralled and enfranchised everywhere, then as now, will scatter flowers and drop tears of gratitude upon the tombs of our fallen heroes, and their names will be held in everlasting remembrance.

Let us never despair of the people of this country. They can endure hardships; they can surmount obstacles; they can toil and suffer and wait. How vivid the recollection to-day, of sacrifices made, of mourning at many hearthstones, of widows clothed in the habiliments of affliction, of the orphan waiting for the father who shall never return. But, thanks be to God! even the eye bedimmed with tears may have glad visions of the future, and the stricken heart find consolation in the assurance that all these sacrifices will be hallowed in

the triumph of freedom and the coming greatness and
glory of our country. Not now

"With trumpet's cry and roll of drums,
This way the tide of battle comes."

but the war is over, and we have celebrated our thanks-
giving to God for deliverance. The greatest crime of
modern times has received its doom, and the enemies
of popular government are justly compelled to accept
terms of readjustment from the prevailing party.

Our eyes now gaze on the grand spectacle of a nation
saved, liberty the birthright of all, a government of the
people and for the people, a government, in which, at
no distant day, not for caste or race or color will any
citizen be debarred from the ballot-box, and against
no child, however lowly or unfortunate, will be closed
the door of the school-house.

Ye down-trodden, give thanks! "Ye shall go out
with joy and be led forth with peace." My fellow citizen—my comrade in arms, be of good cheer. Go forth
to labor, boldly, trustingly. Life's victories are for
those who fight life's battles. There is work for all to
do. There are false principles to uproot, and pernicious
doctrines to correct. Shrink from no duty: evade no
responsibility. True to your manhood—true to the heroic demands of justice and right, be yours the struggle
and yours the glory—

"Heart within and God o'erhead."

The President.—There is another gentleman here who has served the Commonwealth as its Chief Magistrate, and who has richly earned the title bestowed upon him—the Soldier's Friend—Ex-Gov. Smyth, of Manchester. (Cheers.)

SPEECH OF EX-GOV. FREDERICK SMYTH.

Ex-Gov. Smyth thanked the president for introducing him as the soldier's friend; the people for the hearty reception given him, and complimented the Monument and the patriotic spirit which had caused its erection. He then spoke at considerable length of the Homes for disabled volunteer soldiers which had been established at Dayton, Ohio; Milwaukee, Wisconsin, and Augusta, Maine. He spoke of the comforts that had been provided at these Homes for all disabled soldiers who had done honorable service in the war of the rebellion; said they were neither hospitals nor alms-houses, but homes, where subsistence, care, education, religious instruction and employment are provided by the Congress of the United States, to be paid for from forfeitures and fines of deserters from the army. The provision is not a charity. It is a contribution of the bounty-jumpers and bad soldiers to the good and deserving, and is their right. He urged all soldiers who were disabled from earning a living to enter these institutions and enjoy their advantages, as it was not fit that meritorious disabled soldiers should be supported by private or public charity. This speech contained many valuable facts in regard to these institutions, of which the people generally were ignorant.

THE PRESIDENT.—We are rich in the variety and quality of our entertainment; and I have the pleasure now to introduce a gentleman who is serving the State in the Senate of the United States, and who, having apparently suffered somewhat from the chilliness of the day, will doubtless be glad of an opportunity to get warmed up—Senator James W. Patterson.

SPEECH OF SENATOR JAMES W. PATTERSON.

MR. PRESIDENT, LADIES AND GENTLEMEN: At the outbreak and during the pendency of our late civil war, I spoke to the citizens of Claremont of the perils of the government and encouraged your young men to enlist for its defense. In your town hall and on the spot where yon soldier in bronze rests thoughtfully upon his arms, it was my privilege to address you and some now dead, upon the issues of the great struggle.

I know with what patriotic enthusiasm your sons and brothers threw themselves into the conflict; I witnessed with pride, through the weary and painful years of sacrifice, the unflinching devotion of your people at home. Gladly, therefore, did I accept the invitation of our honored Chief Magistrate to participate in these memorial services. I came, however, with no thought to do more than to pay a silent tribute of respect to the memory of the dead. I will detain you therefore for a few moments only, for I can add nothing to the appropriate words of eulogy which have been so eloquently spoken by the accomplished orator of the day.

You have not lifted this impressive statue to its place, to keep watch and ward through the storms of winter and the heats of summer, over the ashes of your fallen children, simply to memorialize their death, for all men die. It is not to perpetuate the heroism with which they fell, for in all your homes, men weak and wasted with the long battle of life, meet death calmly when he comes in his most fearful forms. It is not to exalt the

virtues or the sacrifices of the soldier above those of
the citizen who falls at his task in the conflicts of peace,
and amid the unheralded throng. War, except when
waged to secure or defend some principle essential to
the wellbeing of men, is brutal, and they who voluntarily engage in it from motives of personal aggrandize-
ment, deserve rather the execrations than the gratitude
of their fellows. But our war was to liberate the slave,
and to preserve the integrity of the government.
Your sons fell in the discharge of a great duty. They
gave their lives for the life of the republic. The offering was beautiful and unsullied by any touch of
selfishness.

The brilliant and true-hearted Gardiner and his com-
panions, who sleep in patriot graves, are not here to
solicit honors at your hands, but you rear this memorial
monument that the children of the town, in all their
generations, may remember and emulate the men who
went forth from your companionship and freely gave
their lives to liberty in its terrific but decisive grapple
with arbitrary power.

The allusion of your orator to the numerous enlistments of the men of Claremont in the Second Regiment
of New Hampshire Volunteers, has brought to my
recollection a thrilling incident of the battle of Gettysburg. The New Hampshire Second was under the
command of the youthful Col. Bailey. He was but a
boy in age and appearance, but he handled his regiment
with the coolness and skill of a veteran of a hundred
battles. His subordinate officers were of the same metal
as himself.

Col. Bailey's regiment reached the battle-ground early
on the morning of the second day's fight, and reported to
General Graham, who immediately ordered them to the
support of a battery posted in the famous peach orchard,
which drank the blood of the most terrific carnage of that

day, and through which the tide of battle ebbed and flowed
from morning until night. Late in the afternoon the
battery of Napoleon guns which they had been ordered
to support, having given place to one of rifled guns, the
enemy opened a terrific fire, under cover of which their
infantry advanced from the woods and forced our skir-
mishers back upon the battery. Then it was, that Col.
Bailey solicited the privilege of leading our Second in a
counter charge. The request was granted. Springing to
their feet our men rushed past the battery and hurled
themselves with such irresistible force upon the advancing
foe, as to drive them back within their lines, and then,
posting themselves behind an old rail-fence, held, for a
space, the whole pressure of the rebel front, and when
at last they were compelled by an overwhelming force to
withdraw, leaving three-fifths of their number dead upon
the field, they retreated slowly with banners flying, and
were received back into our lines with loud and long
huzzas, by men who knew the measure of heroic valor in
the peril of battle. Among those who there fought and
fell that day were your sons.

Allusion has also been made to certain invidious com-
parisons which have appeared unfavorable to the Army
of the Potomac. I would utter no word of disparagement
in respect to any portion of the loyal army; but I am sure
the Army of the East has nothing to fear from contrasts.
Unroll the map and read the great battle-names which
became historic in the long struggle, and tell me if the
sons of the east did less bloody and valiant work than
the men of the west. The fires of war that raged all
along our sea-coast were fed by eastern men. Antietam,
Gettysburg, Cedar Mountain and the surrender of Lee,
were in the east, and there they will stand so long as history shall perpetuate our civil conflict. The Army of the
Potomac has nothing to fear from posterity. Its glory
will be uneclipsed in the records of the war.

The stranger who visits St. Paul's Cathedral, reads upon the tomb of the great architect the expressive inscription, "If you seek my monument, look around." *Si monumentum queris circumspice.* These imperishable words might well be written upon our work-shops and court-houses, upon our churches and halls of legislation in commemoration of the men who perished in their defense.

"At Marathon for Greece the Athenians fought," sang the poet Simonides. With equal truth may it be said, that our soldiers fought for the republic and civilization. The statue which we now dedicate with these solemn and appropriate ceremonies, is a fitting and touching tribute from kindred and friends to the brave men who went from your fields and firesides to die for their country; but would we behold their grandest and most enduring monuments, we must look upon the fields and industries which they have helped to open to the free labor of all races; must forecast the comforts of an educated people devoted to the arts of beauty and of profit, and the revenues of a commerce which lays the markets of the world under contribution.

We must contemplate the widening area of the republic dotted with schools and happy homes and thronged by a free, intelligent population, whose national life illustrates the justice of their laws and the purity of their faith.

These are the monuments which their own hands have builded, and they will stand when this which our gratitude has reared shall have crumbled into the dust of ages.

> " Ah, never shall the land forget
> How gushed the life-blood of her brave—
> Gushed warm with hope and courage yet,
> Upon the soil they fought to save ! "

THE PRESIDENT.—Down on the line of the Sugar River Railroad—which you know is soon to be put in operation—in Bradford, lives a gentleman who has ably served the State in the Congress of the United States, and also in the field as commander of the First Regiment of New Hampshire Volunteers— Col. Mason W. Tappan.

SPEECH OF COL. MASON W. TAPPAN.

MR. PRESIDENT, LADIES AND GENTLEMEN: I do not at this late hour propose to detain you with any extended remarks, but I greatly rejoice that it was in my power to be present on this interesting occasion, and to join with the vast throng I see before me in rendering a tribute of grateful respect to the memory of the patriot-dead of old Claremont. It gives me pleasure to see here so many in the old familiar uniforms—the "Boys in Blue;" and I am especially glad to see, by the badges that meet my eye, so many of my brethren of the Grand Army of the Republic, giving an earnest that should treason and rebellion ever again rear their hydra heads, New Hampshire, at least, will not be quite so unprepared to meet them as she was when the last rebellion broke out.

We have assembled here to do honor to the soldiers, both living and dead; and in the few words I shall speak, I cannot help recurring to the cause for which they so nobly fought and died. It was not alone a war for the preservation of the Union, or for the integrity of the Government—important as both those objects were. It was the old struggle over again between the antagonizing forces of liberty and despotism. It was a conflict based on the great idea for which our fathers fought in the Revolution, that all men, of whatever color or race, were created equal and entitled to the enjoyment of life, liberty, and the pursuit of happiness. In other words, it was a conflict for the rights of human nature. And when, after the long and dreary night that had settled down around our armies at the outset of the struggle—with scarcely a star of victory to illumine the gloom—at last, the immor-

tal Proclamation was announced that the clank of a fetter
should never again be heard in all this broad land—how
grandly, how nobly, how cheerfully, did our gallant leaders and our patriot armies accept and vindicate the great
and sublime issue.   And how soon thereafter did the
gloom disperse, and the darkness fade away.   And as the
echo of the last gun died away at Appomattox—when the
last rebel had laid down his arms—when the glorious old
Stars and Stripes—torn, insulted, trampled upon by rebel
hordes once more floated in triumph in every State of the
Union—I thank my God, that the people of this great
country could not only rejoice in a Union, one and indi-
visible—in a Government securely fixed on God's eternal
granite of truth, justice and liberty, but that they could
rejoice also in a nation redeemed, regenerated and disenthralled by the genius of universal emancipation!

It is fitting, then, that you have assembled here almost
in countless numbers, men, women, and children,—on this
anniversary of Sheridan's most glorious victory, to dedicate this beautiful statue, so creditable to the artist, and
to the patriotism and public spirit of the people of this
grand old town.   It is fitting that we raise monuments
of granite, of marble, and of brass to commemorate the
heroic deeds of those who laid down their lives, that—in
the language of the lamented Lincoln—" the Government
of the people, by the people, and for the people might
not perish from the earth."   It is fitting that we make
annual pilgrimages to the hallowed spots where rest the
remains of our citizen soldiers.

      " And Oh ! where can dust to dust be consigned so well,
      As where Heaven its dews shall shed,
      On the martyred patriot's bed,
      And the rocks shall raise their heads of his deeds to tell.'

It is fitting that we go forth annually to strew with
flowers the graves of the noble, and glorious, and patri-

otic dead, that their names and memory may be kept forever green and fragrant, and their priceless achievements handed down to the generations and the ages that are to come after us!

THE PRESIDENT.—Ladies and Gentlemen—I feel very much as though I was in command of a powerful battery—constantly letting off big guns! (Laughter and cheers.) But I have a big gun in reserve, a gentleman who now represents the First New Hampshire District in Congress—Hon. Jacob H. Ela.

SPEECH OF HON. JACOB H. ELA.

It is not without reluctance that I venture to address you in the presence of so many who have earned by their deeds a better right to occupy your time and attention.

I have always felt that it was not only proper but a duty, for each community, in some appropriate manner, to commemorate the individual actions in the great struggle which secured to us nationality, with individual freedom and protection to all beneath the national flag, and the right of the majority to rule through the forms presented by the constitution.

It was no ordinary struggle in which these men engaged, whether we consider their numbers, the fierce stubbornness of the conflict, or the wide-spread influence which it exerted. It was among other things a struggle to maintain the right of a constitutional majority to govern in this nation—to determine whether the voice of the people, constitutionally expressed by a free ballot, was to be respected and obeyed, or whether a minority should revolutionize and destroy the government when they could no longer rule it. It was a rebellion in the interest of slavery and despotism, for no sooner had secession raised its hydra head than it was announced by the Vice-President of the Confederacy, that slavery was to be the corner stone of the governmental structure to come out of it, and the despots of the old world hastened to give it belligerent aid, filled with joy at the seeming prospect of our destruction, and feeling their tottering thrones already more secure. The perjured usurper, who by force and fraud stood over the prostrate form of liberty in France, at once commenced to found a despotism upon our border, upheld by French bayonets, which was announced to be the pioneer movement to bind up the broken fragments of the Latin Races into dynasties for the offshoots of European Royalty.

It was the stunning death-blow which our citizen soldiers planted in the brazen front of rebellion and slavery here, which settled the fate of these prospective Empires on this continent, and sent back the soldiers of France in mortification and disgrace to their humiliated and weakened master, which gave over the Austrian adventurer to his fate, and made the minions of slavery and despotism howl with rage and impotent fury. It was this triumph over rebellion and slavery which kindled the hopes and longing aspirations of Cuba for liberty into efforts to lift the Gem of the Antilles from the thraldom of Spain into the enjoyment of Republican liberty regulated by law— which started the English colonies on the road to independence and annexation. For with independence and freedom for all the people comes one government for this continent. Sooner or later it will come, like the ripened fruit by its own gravitation, if it does not find an earlier harvest.

The influence of our success did not stop on this side of the water. It kindled anew the dying efforts and aspirations of patriots in continental Europe for Republican liberty, and has borne its fruit in revolutions or liberal concession to their demands. Spain has cut off and cast out the gross incubus of Royalty, with which she was encumbered and is struggling for the birth of Republican liberty. England disestablishes her church in Ireland, and Austria liberalizes her Hungarian legislation, while Napoleon, unwillingly and reluctantly surrenders the pre-

rogatives of Empire to quiet the French people, who
by the ballot are recovering a part of what was lost in the
usurpation—recovering it from the reluctant hand which
held the bayonet over prostrate Mexico and uprising
Italy.

What more proper and appropriate then than honors
paid to the memory of those who dared and died in such
a contest. Let them be given, and let their deeds and
names be commemorated in the granite shaft and the
marble column, and in all the other ways which a gener-
ous and a grateful people may suggest, while a nation
saved is the great monument to their united deeds. And
by the memory of the unnumbered whose lives were
given as a sacrifice for our nationality, let us all labor to
extend and perpetuate the ideas of free government and
the principles of liberty for all for which they fought so
well and died so nobly. And among the highest honors
we can bestow is to forget not the duties we owe to the
living friends they left behind. It is by thus honoring
them, we honor ourselves, and make it certain, that if in
the coming generation dangers shall beset our country,
there will not be wanting among our people willing hearts
and strong hands to uphold and protect it.

The President.—I was in hopes to have had the pleasure of introducing to
you Gen. John Bedel, of Bath, but as he has failed to put in an appearance,
we will now close the exercises at the stand by joining, altogether, in that
grand old ascription,

　　　　" Be thou, O God, exalted high,"—

after which the Marshal will re-form the procession.

The procession marched to the Tremont House, where the invited guests,
the committee of arrangements, officers of the day, and citizens, in all about
eighty, ladies and gentlemen, at four o'clock, sat down to a sumptuous dinner.

Members of fire companies and posts of the Grand Army were liberally provided for by contributions of citizens, at the Town Hall, where tables were laid
for about five hundred. After these had eaten, the doors were thrown open to
the multitude. Not less than one thousand persons were fed in this way.
There was a great quantity of food left, which was distributed to such as
needed it.

THE MONUMENT.

The monument consists of a handsome granite pedestal, seven feet high, surmounted by a bronze statue of an infantry volunteer soldier, in full regulation uniform, leaning in an easy and graceful way upon his gun. Beneath the statue, on the granite die, is the following inscription :

ERECTED

IN HONOR OF THE SOLDIERS

OF

CLAREMONT

WHO DIED

IN THE REBELLION OF

1861–5

BY THEIR GRATEFUL

FELLOW CITIZENS.

1869.

FINANCIAL STATEMENT.

RECEIPTS.

E. L. Goddard, for Fourth of July committee of 1865, principal,
    47.00; interest, 13.00,...$60.00
Mrs. E. L. Goddard, Treasurer Auxiliary Sanitary Commission,
    principal, 150.00; interest, 41.25,...191.25
From subscriptions of 1867, principal, 642.72; interest, 95.37,..........738.09
Dramatic company,..94.00
Subscriptions of 1869,..970.63
Town appropriations for Monument and Park Improvement, as per
    vote of 1867–8,..3500.00
                                                                $5553.97

DISBURSEMENTS.

Martin Milmore, for Monument..4000.00
E. Batchelder, for granite curbing,...250.00
Concrete walks and grading,...807.23
Fence, 337.14 ; labor, 159.60,...496.74
                                                                $5553.97

☞ The items of subscriptions and disbursements may be found upon the Town records.

MEMORIAL TABLETS.

The large number of those Claremont men who were killed in battle and died of wounds or disease while in the service, rendered the inscription of their names upon the Monument impracticable; therefore, marble tablets were erected in the Town Hall, bearing the following Roll of Honor—except that the date and manner of the death of each is added here, to perpetuate more fully their record:

Citizen Soldiers of Claremont who died for their Country in the War of the Rebellion, 1861-5.

COLONEL ALEXANDER GARDINER.
Mortally wounded at the battle of Opequan Creek, near Winchester, Va., September 19, 1864. Died of wounds, October 8, 1864.

CAPTAIN WILLIAM HENRY CHAFFIN.
Killed at the battle of Opequan Creek, near Winchester, Va., September 19, 1864.

LIEUTENANT RUEL G. AUSTIN.
Wounded at the battle of Gettysburg, Pa., July 3, 1863. Died of wounds at Baltimore, Md., July 26, 1863.

LIEUTENANT CHARLES O. BALLOU.
Killed at the battle of Fredericksburg, Va., December 13, 1862.

LIEUTENANT ROBERT HENRY CHASE.
Killed at the battle of Ream's Station, Va., August 25, 1864.

LIEUTENANT SAMUEL BROWN LITTLE.
Wounded at the battle of Fredericksburg, Va., December 13, 1862. Died of wounds at Falmouth, Va., December 24, 1862.

LIEUTENANT GEORGE NETTLETON.
Wounded at the battle of Fredericksburg, Va., December 13, 1862. Died of wounds December 23, 1862.

LIEUTENANT HENRY S. PAULL.
Killed at the battle of Opequan Creek, near Winchester, Va., September 19, 1864.

LIEUTENANT WILLIAM DANFORD RICE.
Supposed killed at Poplar Grove Church, Va., September 30, 1864.

DANIEL S. ALEXANDER.*
Killed at the battle of Drury's Bluff, Va., May 13, 1864.

OSCAR C. ALLEN.
Died of disease at Philadelphia, October 2, 1862.

—— * Erroneously cut on tablet, Daniel S. Dickinson.

JAMES P BASCOM.
Died of disease at Falmouth, Va., December 25, 1862.

SAMUEL O. BENTON.
Killed at the battle of Ream's Station, Va., August 16, 1864.

HORACE BOLIO.
Killed at the battle of Gettysburg, Pa., July 2, 1863.

AMOS F. BRADFORD.
Died of Diphtheria, at Paris; Ky., November 10, 1862.

JOSIAH S. BROWN.
Killed at the battle of Fredericksburg, Va., December 13, 1862.

JAMES BURNS.
Killed at the battle of Gettysburg, Pa., July 3, 1863.

CHARLES F. BURRILL.
Killed at the battle of Gettysburg, Pa., July 2, 1863.

CHARLES E. BALLOU.
Died at Washington, D. C., of disease, February 18, 1864.

LUTHER A. CHASE.
Killed at the battle of Fredericksburg, Va., December 13, 1862.

WYMAN R. CLEMENT.
Died of disease, at Washington, D. C., August 1, 1864.

JOSEPH CRAIG.
Killed at the battle of Gettysburg, Pa., July 2, 1863.

ALBERT G. DANE.
Died while prisoner, at Salisbury, N. C., February 3, 1865.

ZIBA L. DAVIS.
Died of disease at Falmouth, Va., January 12, 1863.

JAMES DELMAGE.
Killed at the battle of Fair Oaks, Va., June 1, 1862.

EDWARD E. FRENCH.
Wounded at the battle of Cold Harbor, Va., June 19, 1864. Died of wounds, September 7, 1864.

JOHN GILBERT.
Killed at the battle of Deep Run, Va., Aug. 16, 1864.

FREDERICK W. GODDARD.
Died of disease, at Pemberton Square Hospital, Boston, July 3, 1863.

CHARLES B. GRANDY.
Died of disease, at Washington, D. C., October, 1861.

DAVID H. GRANNIS.
Died of disease at Hilton Head, N. C., March 4, 1863.

CHESTER F. GRINNELS.
Killed at the battle of Fredericksburg, Va., December 13, 1862.

CHARLES A. HART.
Killed at the battle of Fredericksburg, Va., December 13, 1862.

ELISHA M. HILL.
Died of wounds received in battle, October 27, 1862.

DAMON E. HUNTER.
Mortally wounded at the battle of Fair Oaks, Va., June 1, 1862.   Died June 22, 1862.

WILLIAM L. HURD.
Killed at the battle of Lee's Mills, Va., April 16, 1862.

JOHN S. M. IDE.
Killed in an engagement at Yorktown, Va., April 5, 1862.

JOSEPH W. KELLEY.
Died of disease on passage from Fortress Monroe to Washington, in May, 1862.

WALTER B. KENDALL.
Killed in front of Petersburg, Va., June 16, 1864.

J. FISHER LAWRENCE.
Died of disease at Port Royal, S. C., August 8, 1862.

CHARLES B. MARVIN.
Killed at the battle of Antietam, September 17, 1862.

NOAH D. MERRILL.
Died of wounds received in battle, September 16, 1862.

EDWARD F. MOORE.
Killed in the battle of Gettysburg, Pa., July 2, 1863.

HORATIO C. MOORE.
Mortally wounded in the battle of James Island, S. C., June 16, 1862.   Died June 19, 1862.

RANSOM M. NEAL.
Died of disease at Hilton Head, S. C., October 30, 1862.

EVERETT W. NELSON.
Wounded and taken prisoner at Fort Wagner, July 18, 1863.   Died July 24, 1863.

CHARLES H. NEVERS.
Killed in battle at White Oak Swamp, Va., June 30, 1862.

FREDERICK A. NICHOLS.
Mortally wounded near Bermuda Hundred, June 16, 1864.   Died next day.

LYMAN F. PARRISH.
Died of disease at Manchester, N. H., February 20, 1863.

WILLIAM E. PARRISH.
Wounded and taken prisoner in the battle of the Wilderness, and is supposed to have died at Andersonville.

JOEL W. PATRICK.
Died of disease, at Claremont, August 15, 1862.

JOSEPH PENO.
Killed at the battle of James Island, S. C., June 16, 1862.

CHARLES E. PUTNAM.
Killed at the battle of Williamsburg, Va., May 5, 1862.

GEORGE H. PUTNAM.
Killed at the battle of Cold Harbor, Va., June 3, 1864.

GEORGE READ.
Died of disease, at Newark, N. J., September 9, 1862.

HENRY W. PATRICK.
Died of disease, at Claremont, August 20, 1868.

EDGAR T. REED.
Shot while attempting to arrest a deserter, in the autumn of 1864.

WILLIS REDFIELD.
Died of yellow fever, at Newbern, N. C., October 11, 1864.

CHARLES D. ROBINSON.
Killed at the battle of Fredericksburg, Va., December 13, 1862.

GEORGE E. ROWELL.
Died of disease, at Baltimore, Md., April 10, 1864.

GEORGE W. RUSSELL.
Mortally wounded at the battle of Antietam, Va., September 17, 1862, and died next day.

ARD SCOTT.
Taken prisoner at Darbytown, Va., October 1, 1864. Died of starvation and exposure, at Salisbury, N. C., November 20, 1864.

CHARLES N. SCOTT.
Killed at the battle of Fair Oaks, Va., June 1, 1862.

EDWARD E. STORY.
Died of disease, at Hatteras Inlet, March 4, 1862.

ANDREW J. STRAW.
Wounded at the battle of Bull Run, Va., July 21, 1861, and is supposed to have died in the hands of the enemy.

ROLAND TAYLOR.
Mortally wounded at the battle of Gettysburg, Pa., July 2, 1862, and died a few days afterward.

HORACE A. TYRRELL.
Died of disease, on his way home, after discharge, December 30, 1865.

HARVEY M. WAKEFIELD.
Died of disease, July 5, 1862.

GEORGE O. WEBB.
Died of disease, at Camp Fair Oaks, Va., June 15, 1862.

CHARLES W. WETHERBEE.
Killed at the battle of Fair Oaks, Va., June 1, 1862.

JOHN F. WHEELER.
Taken prisoner at the battle of Bull Run, Va., July 21, 1861. Exchanged, and died on shipboard between Salisbury, N. C., and New York.

NORMAN F. WHITMORE.
Died of disease occasioned by wounds, at Jacksonville, Fla., June 9, 1864.

AUGUSTUS E. WOODBURY.
Taken prisoner at Olustee, Fla., February 10, 1864, died at Andersonville, Ga., June 23, 1864.

SAMUEL S. CARLETON.
Died at Claremont, January 23, 1867, of wounds received in battle.

www.ingramcontent.com/pod-product-compliance
Lightning Source LLC
Chambersburg PA
CBHW031819090426
42739CB00008B/1343